God Speaks About You!

by: Erica Giesow

Illustrator: Ed Koehler

SPEAK**it**BOOKS.org

Pulbished by: Speak it Books
speakitbooks.org

ISBN-13: 978-0615592657
ISBN-10: 0-61559-265-1

a special gift
for a special kid

To: Our Princess Kali-Co

Love
From: Oma & Papa

Date: December 24, 2012

We are so glad you
have Jesus in your
heart Kali. Remember He is
your bestfriend!
We are so proud of you.
Kiss Kiss

{ Ella Joy }
May you never forget
all the things God speaks about You!
We love you always!

You are favored and blessed.

Your life will be full of the very best.

you will surely live long.

You are
loved and adored.

God's plans are for you to soar!

You are joyful & smart.

And God lives in your heart.

Angels are commanded to guard you.

And Jesus' blood protects and surrounds you.

Your spirit is keen.

On God's voice you will lean.

your body is complete,

from your head

down to your feet.

Your soul
is well.

In His presence you will dwell.

God's
Word
is in
your
heart,

and from it
you will never depart.

You are anointed and graced.

With endurance you will finish your race.

God speaks it.
We repeat it.

And with all our heart,
we believe it.

Scripture References

You are **FAVORED** and **BLESSED**. Your life will be **FULL of the very BEST!**

> Psalm 5:12 (NIV): For surely, O Lord, you bless the righteous; you surround them with your favor as with a shield.
> Psalm 34:10 (NIV): But those who seek the LORD lack no good thing.

You are **HEALTHY** and **STRONG**. You will surely **LIVE LONG**.

> 1 Peter 2:24 (NIV): By His wounds we have been healed.
> Psalm 91:16 (NIV): With long life will I satisfy him and show him my salvation.

You are **LOVED** and **ADORED.** God's **PLANS** are for **YOU TO SOAR!**

> Jeremiah 31:3 (NIV): The LORD appeared to us in the past, saying: "I have loved you with an everlasting love; I have drawn you with loving-kindness."
> Jeremiah 29:11 (NIV): "For I know the plans I have for you," declares the LORD, "plans to prosper you and not to harm you, plans to give you hope and a future."

You are **JOYFUL & SMART.** And **GOD LIVES IN YOUR HEART**.

> 1 Peter 1:8 (NIV): You believe in Him and are filled with an inexpressible and glorious joy.
> 1 Corinthians 2:16 (NIV): But we have the mind of Christ.
> 1 Corinthians 6:19 (NIV): Your body is a temple of the Holy Spirit, who is in you.

Angels are **COMMANDED** to **GUARD** you and Jesus' blood **PROTECTS** and **SURROUNDS** you.

> Psalm 91:11 (NIV): For He will command his angels concerning you to guard you in all your ways.
> Exodus 12:23 (NIV): He will see the blood on the top and sides of the doorframe and will pass over that doorway, and he will not permit the destroyer to enter your houses and strike you down.
> Hebrews 9:12 (NIV): He did not enter by means of the blood of goats and calves; but he entered the Most Holy Place once for all by his own blood, having obtained eternal redemption.

Your **SPIRIT** is **KEEN.** On **GOD'S VOICE** you will **LEAN.**

John 14:17 (NIV): The Spirit of truth. The world cannot accept him, because it neither sees him nor knows him. But you know him, for he lives with you and will be in you.

John 10:27 (NIV): My sheep listen to my voice; I know them, and they follow me.

Your **BODY** is **COMPLETE,** from your **HEAD** down to **YOUR FEET!**

1 Peter 2:24 (NIV): By His wounds we have been healed.

Proverbs 4:20 & 22 (NIV): Listen closely to my words...for they are life to those who find them and health to a man's whole body.

Your **SOUL** is **WELL.** In **HIS PRESENCE** you will **DWELL.**

3 John 1:2 (NIV): Dear friend, I pray that you may enjoy good health and that all may go well with you, even as your soul is getting along well.

Psalm 23:6 (NIV): I will dwell in the house of the Lord forever.

GOD'S WORD is in your **HEART,** and from it you will **NEVER DEPART.**

Jeremiah 31:33 (NIV): I will put my law in their minds and write it on their hearts.

Proverbs 22:6 (NIV): Train a child in the way he should go, and when he is old he will not turn from it.

You are **ANOINTED** and **GRACED.** With endurance you will **FINISH YOUR RACE.**

1 John 2:27 (NIV): As for you, the anointing you received from him remains in you.

1 Timothy 1:14 (NIV): The grace of our Lord was poured out on me abundantly.

2 Timothy 4:7 (NIV): I have fought the good fight, I have finished the race, I have kept the faith.

God **SPEAKS IT.** We **REPEAT IT.** And with all our **HEART,** we **BELIEVE IT!**

2 Corinthians 4:13 (NIV): It is written: "I believed; therefore I have spoken." With that same spirit of faith we also believe and therefore speak.

Mark 11:23-24 (NIV): "I tell you the truth, if anyone says to this mountain, 'Go, throw yourself into the sea,' and does not doubt in his heart but believes that what he says will happen, it will be done for him. Therefore I tell you, whatever you ask for in prayer, believe that you have received it, and it will be yours."